VIOLIN SCALE TALES

Fun-to-Play Etudes in First Position

ELAINE FINE

WWW.MELBAY.COM

Introduction

Practicing scales is important for building and maintaining technique, gaining bow control, improving intonation, developing strength, and acquiring a vibrant and varied sound. But for many students, practicing scales feels like a chore, particularly in the keys that have more than three sharps or flats; these scales are challenging because the musical territory is unfamiliar.

This book offers students who have not yet learned to shift above first position a musically and intellectually engaging way of practicing scales in all of the major and minor keys. These one-page lyrical compositions move up and down stepwise in each of the major and minor keys, with pitch repetition only at the unison and the octave. This stepwise motion makes the distance from one pitch to the next easy to hear and feel, even when playing in keys filled with many sharps or flats. Ample fingerings are provided for the passages that necessitate half position.

The title of each etude refers to an animal that has scales. The minor scales are named after twelve interesting and beautiful varieties of moths, and the major scales are named for turtles, lizards, birds, an armadillo, a snake, and a flying squirrel. The order follows the circle of fifths, with a mixture of natural and harmonic minor scales preceding their relative majors. The book ends with etudes that travel through all the major and minor keys. These scale etudes can also be played using a mixture of positions by advanced players, and they sound very resonant when played at pitch on the viola. The etudes can also be performed as solo pieces.

I enjoyed learning about the behavior, movement, and appearance of these animals while writing these pieces and, and I hope that practicing these pieces and learning about these animals will spark the creative imaginations of people who play them. They might even be inspired to try their hands at writing scale pieces of their own.

Elaine Fine

Contents

Atlas Moth

Attacus atlas

A minor

Elaine Fine

Green Sea Turtle

Chelonia mydas

C major

Elephant Hawk Moth

Deilephila elpenor

E minor

Ostrich

Struthio camelus

G major

Io Moth

Automeris io

B minor

Con fuoco

Komodo Dragon

Varanus komodoensis

D major

Rosy Maple Moth

Dryocampa rubicunda

F-sharp minor

Screaming Hairy Armadillo

Chaetophractus vellerosus

A major

Luna Moth

Actis luna

C-sharp minor

Emu

Dromaius novaehollandiae

E major

Garden Tiger Moth

Arctia caja

G-sharp minor

The harmonics are played by touching the single fourth finger lightly on the string, and moving a very straight bow firmly and quickly. The sound comes out an octave higher than printed. If there is no harmonic indicated, just apply the fourth finger normally.

Armadillo Girdled Lizard

Ouroborus cataphractus

B major

Dysphania Militaris Moth

Dysphania militaris

D-sharp minor

Eastern Collared Lizard

Crotaphytus collaris

F-sharp major

This piece can also be played in F major as well by replacing the six sharps in the key signature with a single B flat.

Cecropia Giant Silk Moth

Hyalophora cecropia

B-flat minor

Royal Python

Python regius

D-flat major

Twin-Spotted Sphinx Moth

Simerinthus Jamaicensis

F minor

Barred Owl

Strix Varia

A-flat major

Comet Moth

Argema mittrei

C minor

Dwarf Scaly-Tailed Squirrel

Anomalurus pusillis

E-flat major

Cinnabar Moth

Tyria jacobaeae

G minor

Galápagos Tortoise

Chelonoidis nigra

B-flat major

Giant Leopard Moth

Hypercompre scribonia

D minor

Scaly-Breasted Woodpecker

Celeus grammicus

F major

Waltz of the Emus

A journey through all the major keys

97
104
111
118
127
135
142
148
157
164
171
177
184

Waltz of the Moths

A journey through all the minor keys

129
138
149
159
167
175
185
195
204
214
225
235
246

257
266
274
283
293
302
313
323
333
343
353
363
374